PREHISTORIC LIFE

THE FIRST SETTLEMENTS

RUPERT MATTHEWS

Illustrated by Bernard Long

The Bookwright Press
New York • 1990

Titles in this series

How Life Began
The Dinosaur Age
The Age of Mammals

Ice Age Animals
The First People
The First Settlements

Front cover illustration: Early people built simple wooden shelters in an area that was easy to defend.

First published in the United States by
The Bookwright Press
387 Park Avenue South
New York NY 10016

First published in 1990 by
Wayland (Publishers) Ltd
61 Western Road, Hove
East Sussex, BN3 1JD, England

Library of Congress Cataloging-in-Publication Data
Matthews, Rupert
    The first settlements/by Rupert O. Matthews
        p. cm. – (Prehistoric life)
    Bibliography: p.
    Includes index.
    Summary: Surveys early periods of human history and settlement from hunting and gathering to farming to the development of metals and the establishment of the first cities.
    ISBN 0-531-18299-1
    1. Man, Prehistoric – Juvenile literature. 2. Human settlements – History – Juvenile literature. (1. Man, Prehistoric. 2. Human settlements – History.) I. Title. II. Series: Matthews, Rupert. Prehistoric life.
GN744.M37 1990
930.1 – dc 19   89-30634
                                                    CIP
                                                    AC

Typeset by Direct Image Photosetting Ltd.,
Hove, East Sussex, England
Printed by G. Canale & C.S.p.A., Turin, Italy

Contents

Words printed in **bold** are explained in the glossary.

The Hunting Peoples

Until about 10,000 BC humans did not lead a settled life. Instead of having a home and living in one place, people moved around throughout the year. They did so because they were continually searching for food. At that time people did not know how to grow **crops** or raise animals. They had to catch wild animals and collect fruit, nuts and other plant food. Such a lifestyle is called "hunter-gatherer." Because these people ate all the food available in one place fairly quickly, they needed to move on frequently. This life of constant movement is known as "nomadic." Even today some groups of people, such as the **Bushmen** of Africa and a few Australian **Aborigines**, lead a nomadic hunter-gatherer life.

Because these people lived an unsettled life did not mean that they were uncultured. The **Paleolithic** period, or Old Stone Age, was a time of great artistic expression. Some bands always spent the winter or summer in a particular place. A few caves in Europe were decorated with magnificent paintings of wild animals. The paintings were done by Paleolithic people who stayed in the caves from time to time.

Left The pictures in the Lascaux Caves in France were painted by Paleolithic people.

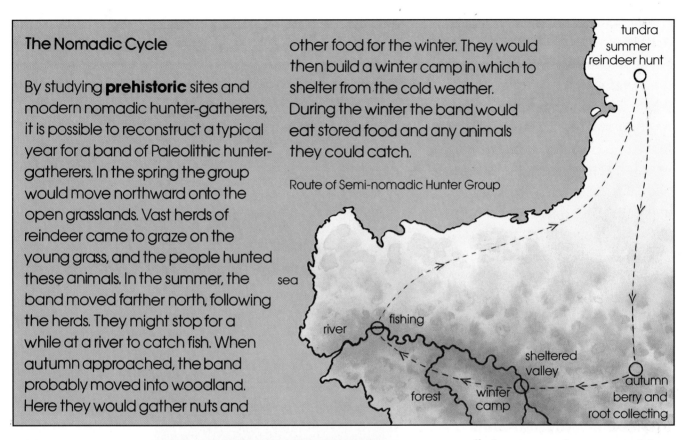

The Nomadic Cycle

By studying **prehistoric** sites and modern nomadic hunter-gatherers, it is possible to reconstruct a typical year for a band of Paleolithic hunter-gatherers. In the spring the group would move northward onto the open grasslands. Vast herds of reindeer came to graze on the young grass, and the people hunted these animals. In the summer, the band moved farther north, following the herds. They might stop for a while at a river to catch fish. When autumn approached, the band probably moved into woodland. Here they would gather nuts and other food for the winter. They would then build a winter camp in which to shelter from the cold weather. During the winter the band would eat stored food and any animals they could catch.

Route of Semi-nomadic Hunter Group

tundra
summer
reindeer hunt

sea

river   fishing

forest   winter camp   sheltered valley

autumn berry and root collecting

Right These stone blades, or knives, were made by prehistoric people.

Left A group of hunter-gatherers move through the forest in search of a clearing to camp for the night.

Some everyday objects of these people were beautifully decorated. Spears and other weapons were engraved with pictures and some people wore jewelry. The nomadic hunter-gatherers could even make and play musical instruments.

To help them capture animals the Paleolithic peoples made many weapons. Sharp spearheads and arrowheads were made from flint or other stone. Bone was used to make barbed fishing spears and harpoons. Other tools were used to cut up carcasses and to convert skin into leather or fur clothes. Some specialized tools were used to gather vegetables and to process them. The tools and artistic talents of these people came together to form a fine culture.

The First Crops

About 12,000 BC the **climate** of the entire world began to change. The **Ice Age** was coming to an end. The massive **glaciers** which covered mountains such as the Alps in Europe, and blanketed much of the northern half of the world, began to melt. Scientists are not quite certain why this happened, but it had a dramatic effect throughout the world.

The melting ice raised the level of the oceans. One consequence of this was that Britain became an island. Throughout the world the climate became warmer and drier. This gradual change produced problems for the hunter-gatherers. In some areas summers became hot and dry instead of warm and moist. Plants died off and food

became difficult to find. The local people had to find another source of food. Some moved to different areas while others concentrated on activities such as fishing. However, a few groups of people started a very different kind of life; they began to cultivate crops.

Above Most of the northern half of the world must have looked similar to this during the Ice Age.

This cultural change first occurred in the Near East, in the modern countries of Iraq, Israel and Syria. The switch from hunting and gathering to farming probably happened very slowly. The people at the time may not have realized what an important event this was.

The people of the area would have been familiar with certain grasses that grew around them. These plants flourished in large masses and produced big seeds. Such plants have been identified by **archaeologists** as wild wheat and

Above A field of wheat and wild oats ripening in the summer sun.

wild barley. When the seeds, or grain, were collected they could be ground between two stones and boiled to make a type of porridge. As hunter-gatherers, the people of the area probably made use of this grain in the autumn.

Gradually, people realized that the grain could be collected and stored. It could then be used as food throughout the winter months when little fresh food was available. If stored properly, the grain could be kept into the following summer as well. Such grain stores probably developed only slowly. They may have been kept at a special site while the hunter-gatherers moved off in search of food. Only if they failed to find enough to eat would the band return to use the grain store. In this way, humans might have become increasingly dependent on the supply of grain.

Below These hunting people have stopped to pick some wild grain.

Domesticating Animals

Scientists still argue about the early **domestication** of animals. Nobody can be quite certain when it first happened, nor which creatures were involved.

For many millions of years humans hunted animals for food.

During all this time they made no attempt whatsoever to tame their **prey**. The creatures moved and behaved as they wished. The humans simply hunted them by lying in wait or setting traps for the animals.

Below It is not easy to tame wild animals. These men are trying to catch some sheep.

Above The Lapps of Scandinavia still keep herds of reindeer as domestic animals.

It is possible that some bands of Paleolithic hunters practiced a type of semi-domestication. They may have attached themselves to particular herds of animals. The band would follow this herd all year, killing animals whenever they wished. However, the Paleolithic people made no attempt to control either the movements or the breeding of the animals although they lived in close contact.

At some time, however, a closer association between humans and animals began. Perhaps the people following a herd penned some animals into a certain area so that they would be easier to catch. These animals would gradually become used to their human masters and could be called **domestic animals**.

It is hard to be certain whether a bone came from a wild animal or a domestic one. However, there are some clues; most scientists agree that while hunters kill wild animals of all ages, people who keep domestic animals prefer the meat of young, tender animals. When scientists **excavate** a site they keep a record of the age of animals whose bones they find. If they dig up many bones from young animals, it is assumed that they were domestic animals.

On this basis, archaeologists estimate that goats and sheep were domesticated about 7000 BC, and cattle about 500 years later.

The Domestic Horse

Paleolithic carvings of horses from France have led some researchers to suggest that this animal was domesticated some time around 30,000 years ago. Some of these carvings show what appear to be leather **bridles** around the horses' heads. However, other scientists believe the markings merely show hair. They suggest that the horse was first domesticated in the USSR about 4000 BC.

Early Farmers

By about 8000 BC the use of grain together with domestic animals brought about the appearance of the first true farmers. These people lived in permanent villages, which were inhabited throughout the year.

In the spring the farmers would sow grain in the fields around the village. During the summer the wheat or barley would grow. By the autumn, the grain was ripe and ready for harvesting. The farmers used **sickles** made of small flint blades set in long wooden handles to harvest the grain. The stems were cut with the sickle and the grain heads collected. Later the grain was separated from the stalks and chaff by **threshing**.

Herds of domestic goats and sheep were kept in the same village. Herders would take the animals out to graze on nearby grasslands. At night the flocks might be driven into enclosures where they would be safe from wild animals.

Gradually the types of grain and animals improved. The herders soon learned that large animals tend to produce large young. They began to control the breeding of the domestic animals. Only robust goats were allowed to breed, since they produced domestic animals much stronger and larger than those in the wild. The farmers also began to sow grains that would give bigger and better harvests.

At first the farming villages existed only in hill country where there was enough rain to allow wheat and barley to grow. However, as populations increased, villages began to appear in river valleys. The farmers of these villages had to carry water from the river to their crops at dry times of the year. Some of these early villages were surrounded by strong walls. Perhaps the farmers sometimes found themselves under attack from hunter-gatherers who wanted to steal food.

Below In about 6000 BC a village in the Near East might have looked like this.

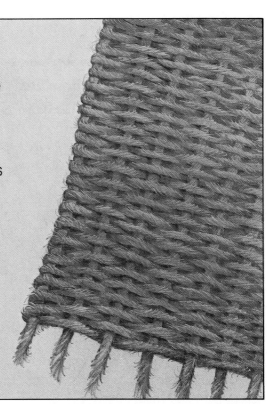

New Types of Clothing

During the Paleolithic period people wore clothes made out of leather and furs. These were very warm and useful, and were skillfully sewn together. However, the early farmers wore entirely different types of clothing. The wool that they cut from domestic sheep and goats was carefully gathered and spun into thread. This thread could then be woven into cloth. Exactly when people began wearing woolen cloth is not known, but they were certainly doing so by about 6000 BC.

Farming in Europe

Farming began in the Near East for two reasons. First, in this area there was a great need to find new sources of food. Second, there was plenty of grain growing wild in the Near East.

However, once people began to farm they quickly realized that more food could be produced from a small area of land than by hunter-gatherer techniques. Growing crops was also a better way of ensuring a food supply than searching for wild foods. The practice of farming spread rapidly. Scientists are not certain exactly how this happened. It might be that bands of hunter-gatherers learned about farming from other groups. Or possibly people from a farming community moved into lands not previously farmed where they pushed the hunter-gatherers out.

By whatever method farming spread, it rapidly came to be practiced over a wide area.

Below It was in Greece that scientists found the earliest signs of domesticated cattle. In the background, crops (wheat or barley) are being harvested.

The First Pottery

It was while farming was spreading through Europe that pottery was first produced. With pots, bowls and plates, people were able to store and cook food more efficiently. The earliest known pottery comes from Iran and was made in about 7000 BC. These pots were not very well made and were easily broken. As potters became more skilled they were able to produce larger pieces in a variety of shapes. Once invented, this technique spread quickly, and pottery was soon being used by farmers in most areas.

It spread to parts of southern Europe, where the climate was similar to that in the Near East. It was in Greece and Turkey, for instance, that scientists found the earliest signs of domesticated cattle. Farming was restricted to these areas because wheat and barley would not grow in the cooler, wetter climate farther north.

However, the farmers living on the edge of the areas of suitable climate began to develop strains of grain that were better suited to local conditions. These farmers were then able to move farther north until the new strains of wheat could no longer grow. In years to come, farmers in these areas would develop even more resistant strains and so push a little farther north. By about 4000 BC farming was being practiced in the Danube Basin. About a thousand years later the lands of Germany, France and Britain were being farmed.

The Standing Stones

Before the invention of farming, people had needed to spend nearly all their time searching for food. However, agriculture is a seasonal lifestyle. A lot of work needed to be done during the spring plowing and the autumn harvest, but between these seasons farmers had time for other occupations. In some areas they spent their spare time on **irrigation** projects, or on building defensive walls. In northwest Europe, however, the people made huge monuments which remain standing today as magnificent **memorials** to the past.

The most spectacular of these structures is Stonehenge, in Wiltshire, England. Here more than 160 massive boulders, some weighing many tons, were carefully shaped and then set upright. Some of the stones were hoisted to lie across the tops of others. The **concentric** circles of Stonehenge were laid out to a precise plan. The whole structure is a great triumph of ancient engineering.

A few miles to the north of Stonehenge stand the remains of another massive stone monument. This is the complex of Avebury. The central monument covers 25 acres and contained a circle of 100 upright stones with an average

Above Only parts of Stonehenge remain standing today.

weight of 15 tons. Eighty other stones stood in smaller circles within the structure while some 400 uprights formed avenues leading to Avebury. The great circle was surrounded by a long, massive ditch and bank 16 m (52 ft) from top to bottom.

Hundreds of smaller stone circles and other erections are to be found in Britain and France.

Nobody is certain why they were built. The effort required to assemble such large stones must have been huge. Hundreds of men would have labored for many years to construct the larger circles.

Some scientists think the stone circles were **temples** of some kind. They imagine mysterious ceremonies being carried out by priests and farmers. Others think that the stones formed a type of calendar. Some of the stones line up with sunrise or sunset on certain days of the year. Perhaps this told the farmers when it was time to plant their crops. It may be that the prehistoric builders had both purposes in mind. Or they may have had reasons at which we cannot even guess.

Below It took a tremendous amount of hard work to erect each stone of the Avebury Circle.

15

Rice Cultures

In the Near East and Europe the hardships caused by the end of the Ice Age led to the development of an agriculture based on wheat, barley, sheep and goats. Elsewhere in the world other groups of people faced similar hardships. However, these peoples were not fortunate enough to have wild wheat and barley which they could use in agriculture.

In Southeast Asia, however, there was a very different wild grain which came to be used as a food source. This was rice, which grew in hot, damp areas. The cultivation of rice probably began in much the same way as the cultivation of grain in the Near East. Bands of hunter-gatherers would have become familiar with

Above This village in Thailand is similar to an ancient rice village.

Below In Asia, early farmers domesticated the wild pig.

rice as a food source. Later they would have learned how to plant the seeds and then harvest the crop. As the years passed, the strains of rice were gradually improved.

The very earliest traces of rice being deliberately grown by humans date back to about 6000 BC in eastern China. Scientists have also found evidence of early rice cultivation in what is now Thailand. The early farmers who grew rice also cultivated other plants such as peppers and pumpkin-like gourds. One of the few animals suitable for domestication in the area was the pig. This animal has the advantage of producing many young which put on weight very quickly.

The Cultivation of Rice

Rice is a grain crop which demands special care if it is to be grown successfully. It is a swamp plant, so fields have to imitate the conditions of a swamp. A field is prepared by spreading a layer of soil over waterproof clay and surrounding it by an earthen bank. The field is then flooded with water. The young rice plants, which have been **germinated** in special seedling beds, are placed in the flooded soil. The water is kept circulating to prevent it going stale, which would

kill the rice. Throughout the growing season, the fields are kept flooded. When the rice plant reaches a height of about 1.2 m (4 ft) the seeds begin to form. The water is then drained off to allow the rice grains to ripen quickly.

The agricultural system based on growing rice and keeping pigs spread rapidly through Southeast Asia. Within a few centuries, rice was being grown in India. However, scientists are not certain whether cultivated rice was brought to these areas from Southeast Asia or whether it already grew there wild and was cultivated independently.

Rice was a good food source for early hunter-gatherers.

Prehistoric China

The earliest signs of agriculture in China date back to about 5000 BC. Scientists have named this early culture the Yang-shao. As with other early farming cultures, the Yang-shao was based on the plants that grew wild in the area. Clustered around the middle reaches of the Yangtse River, the farmers of the Yang-shao grew millet as their main crop. Once harvested, the grain was ground between two stones to make flour, which could then be used in a variety of ways. The domesticated animals were pigs and dogs, both of which were eaten.

An important Yang-shao site has recently been discovered at Banpo. The Banpo village has been fully excavated and has revealed much about the physical culture of the earliest Chinese. The settlement contained about 600 people and was surrounded by a massive ditch. Presumably, the people of Banpo were afraid of being attacked.

Below This is how the village of Banpo may have looked.

Tools such as spades, hoes and digging sticks were used to farm the millet fields that surrounded the village. A nearby river provided the Banpo people with plenty of fish. Many clay pots and jugs were found. There was a high quality black pottery for important occasions and a cheaper gray pottery for everyday use.

About 3000 BC a new culture appeared in China. Scientists have named this the Lung-shan culture. This was more advanced with a greater range of crops and more inventions. The Lung-shan grew rice as well as millet. They kept sheep, horses and cattle in addition to pigs, which gave them a more varied diet.

The Lung-shan people had developed the potter's wheel. With this simple invention they could produce high quality pottery that was suitable for a very wide range of uses. The extremely successful Chinese **ceramic** industry can be dated from this time.

Another industry which made its first appearance among the Lung-shan was the weaving of silk. Silkworms were kept and raised by villagers of this period. The fine silk was used to make clothes which may have been worn by important people such as village chiefs.

The Lung-shan culture continued to develop and improve over the following centuries. Gradually it spread out from its original home in the Yangtse Basin to the Hwang-Ho River and surrounding lands. In about 1650 BC the culture emerged from prehistory when the Shang Dynasty formed the earliest known Chinese Empire.

The Pacific

Throughout millions of years of **evolution** humans could not cross large bodies of water. They swam short distances across water, but wider rivers and oceans were barriers to their movements. About 50,000 years ago people discovered a method of crossing wide stretches of water. In doing so they opened up the vast lands of the Pacific Ocean to human occupation.

It seems that the first people to cross the ocean were the ancestors of the Australian Aborigines. **Fossil** bones found on Borneo show that prehistoric Australian people lived there some 40,000 years ago. Fifteen thousand years later humans had reached the Philippines. To arrive on these islands, the newcomers needed to cross ocean straits from 80 to 150 km (50 to 90 mi) wide. We do not know exactly how these voyages were made, but it seems most likely that the early Australians made canoes out of hollowed logs.

Today, their descendants live in Australia and New Guinea. The vast majority of these peoples lived a hunter-gatherer way of life before the arrival of Europeans about 300 years ago. It would appear that the early Australians had not invented agriculture when they undertook their ocean crossings.

Left Solomon Island fishermen head out to sea in their dug-out canoe.

Far left The first canoes were made by hollowing out the trunk of a tree. Some canoes are still made this way today.

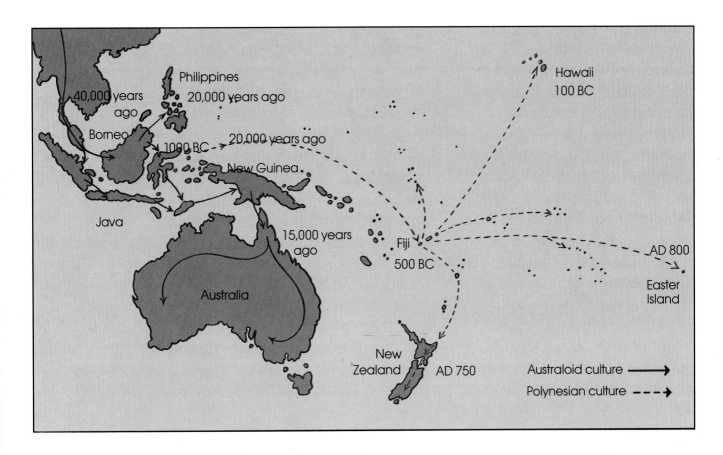

Above This map shows the spread of the Polynesians throughout the Pacific.

Many years after the prehistoric Australians crossed the ocean, a new wave of humans spread across the Pacific from Asia. These were the Polynesians — people who today inhabit many islands spread across thousands of square miles of ocean. The Polynesians were able to build extremely fine canoes in which they could travel hundreds of miles. They were also highly-skilled **navigators** and were able to find a small island even after a voyage of several days.

The Polynesians were farmers who grew crops well suited to their home islands. The tropical yam and taro plants, with large edible roots, provided them with most of their nutrition. Pigs were kept in large numbers, and in some areas a person's wealth was counted in swine. Many different types of fruit could be gathered from the forests that covered the Pacific islands. The eastward movement of the Polynesians may have begun about 1000 BC, and they could have reached Fiji by 500 BC. In about AD 750 the first Polynesian **Maoris** reached New Zealand, where they settled.

The Americas

Until about 30,000 years ago no human beings lived in North America or South America. The evolution of humans had taken place in Africa, Europe and Asia. The Americas were separated from those lands by wide oceans, so early people could not reach the new continents. However, about 28,000 years ago the sea level dropped as vast amounts of water froze to form the glaciers of the Ice Age. The falling sea revealed a bridge of dry land between Siberia and Alaska. Bands of people migrated across this bridge.

These humans were hunter-gatherers. They followed herds of animals into Alaska and then traveled south. The first people reached Mexico about 20,000 years ago and the southern tip of South America about 10,000 years later. For many centuries the people remained hunter-gatherers. In some areas, such as the North American plains, this way of life was unchanged until the arrival of Europeans about 400 years ago.

About 2500 BC some bands of people in the Americas began to abandon hunter-gathering in favor of raising crops. This probably first happened in Mexico. Elsewhere the change was dependent on the types of edible plants available for farming.

Below In South America, early civilizations built magnificent temples where they worshiped their gods.

The early Mexicans had a wide range of plants to choose from. They could grow avocados, beans, chili peppers, corn, pumpkins and cacti.

At first all these plants were cultivated. As the years passed, however, some plants developed strains which gave heavier crops, while others remained unchanged. The farmers gradually came to concentrate on corn, avocados and chilis. By about 1300 BC the people of Mexico had developed pottery. Their population was growing and, although they still lived in scattered villages, the people came together for religious purposes. Massive stone temples were built, and some remain standing to this day.

Farther south, in the Andes Mountains of South America, a different form of agriculture was developed. Here the chief crops were potatoes, sweet potatoes and corn. Ducks and guinea pigs were kept as food while llamas were kept for wool. Here too, the culture eventually gave rise to complex civilizations which built mighty temples and large cities. In North America the Mississippi valley became the center for an agricultural system based on corn and pumpkin-like squashes.

The First Metals

By 6000 BC humans had been making weapons and tools from stone and bone for many thousands of years. At about that time an entirely new material began to come into use. It improved human civilization enormously and people were able to make much better tools and weapons. The new material was metal.

The very first metals to be made into **artifacts** were gold and copper. Both these metals occur naturally in small lumps, or nuggets. These nuggets can be shaped by hammering into various designs. Gold ornaments and small copper pins or tools were being produced in the Middle East by about 6000 BC. However, the uses of such small objects were limited.

In about 4000 BC someone made a remarkable discovery. If certain types of rock were placed around a camp-fire, small amounts of copper would run out and solidify. When larger amounts of the rock were pounded to powder and placed in a pottery kiln, large pieces of copper were produced. This process, of grinding and heating ore to produce metal, is known as smelting. It allowed the prehistoric metal workers to produce metal more quickly and more cheaply.

Below An early metal worker puts crushed rocks into a pot to be placed in the hot kiln.

Soon after the discovery of copper smelting, it was found that if small amounts of tin were added to the copper a new **alloy** was produced. This was bronze, and it had several advantages over copper. Bronze is harder than copper, and it is easier to cast. Casting is the process by which molten metal is poured into a mold and allowed to cool. It then takes on the shape of the mold. Many objects, such as hammers, knives and axes can be made in this way. Early molds were open on one side, which made the work of casting easier.

However, using open molds meant that only a limited range of shapes could be cast. Later smiths used two-part molds. These were bound together before the molten metal was poured. Once the metal was cool, the two parts of the mold were separated, leaving the object behind. This process greatly increased the number of tools that could be made by casting.

Metal had many advantages over stone or bone. It was harder and lasted longer than other materials. It could easily be repaired – a blunt knife can be sharpened, for example, or melted down to make another tool. Metal quickly took over from stone as the basic material for tool production.

The Changing Society

Alongside the technological advances being made by early farmers, changes in society were occurring. Some of the earliest farmers were forced to build defenses around their villages to protect themselves from attack. As methods of farming improved, more food could be produced from the same patch of land. This meant that more people could live in a village.

As time passed some of these villages grew to be very large indeed. Jericho, in Palestine, had a population of around 3,000 people and covered an area of nearly 10 acres. Such a large and prosperous village was an obvious target for attack by other farmers or nomads who were not so successful. The people of Jericho built massive walls, with watchtowers about 10 m (32 ft) tall, to protect themselves.

Within these large villages society was changing. As hunter-gatherers and primitive farmers, all the people of a band had needed to cooperate to produce enough food. Everyone had to help plant seeds and harvest crops or they would starve. However, as more food was produced for less effort, some people could afford not to work on farms at all. If these people could produce goods needed by the farmer, they could swap, or barter, them for food.

Below A farmer offers a basket of grain in exchange for a few pots.

In this way, specialization of industry began to take place. Some people would spend all their time making pottery or metal tools. The pots or tools would then be exchanged for food. This was a major advance for it allowed skilled professionals to concentrate on skilled trades. Even better tools were produced for the farmers to use on the land.

Soon other specialists joined the craftspeople as non-farmers within the villages. Among the first to appear were merchants. They would travel from village to village buying and selling goods. For instance one village might have a particularly skillful potter. A merchant would buy pots from this person and take them to a nearby village. Here the pots would be sold for a profit. Such trade was carried out by barter. About 3200 BC writing was invented. People could now keep written accounts of their property and business deals. Soon scribes, people who could read and write, made a living by their skill.

The First Cities

The changing societies of the larger farming villages were slowly developing into true towns. The final step to an **urban** environment was first taken in the valley of the Euphrates and the Tigris, the twin rivers of Mesopotamia. The change was brought about by two main factors.

The first of these was the invention of the ox-drawn plow. With a plow, one person could farm a much larger area of land than before. This meant that there was a large surplus of food to support the activities of more specialized workers. The highly **fertile** land of Mesopotamia encouraged this development.

The second factor was the development of irrigation. Although the soil was fertile, it was difficult to farm. The rivers tended to flood in the spring when the farmers should have been planting seed. Through the rest of the year the river levels fell, robbing the fields of much-needed moisture. The answer to these problems was irrigation. Large mounds of earth on the river banks prevented the spring floods. Long ditches carrying water from the rivers to the fields provided water for the growing crops.

Below The king and his party stop to watch some workers digging an irrigation ditch.

The Fertile Crescent

The farmers of the Near East lived on the fertile lands that reached along the river valleys of the Euphrates, Tigris, Jordan and Nile. These valleys form the shape of a giant crescent. Within this Fertile Crescent, as it is known, many crucial developments in the history of civilization took place.

Such irrigation projects could not be built effectively by individual farmers. People had to work together to produce efficient systems. Such cooperation demanded central authority of some kind. It was this need that gave rise to the first kings and rulers of the ancient world. Their most important task was to ensure that the irrigation system was properly maintained.

With the great advantages of irrigation, even more food surpluses were produced. Some of this was taken by the king in the form of taxes to pay for irrigation projects. The rest was sold by the farmer in exchange for goods that he needed but could not make himself. At the heart of such a system was the king and his court, surrounded by large numbers of specialized workers. These people joined together to live in a city in the middle of the land controlled by the king.

By 2700 BC some cities had reached a large size. They covered many acres of land and were surrounded by massive **fortifications**. Society had changed totally to produce urban people. The modern social pattern had begun.

Glossary

Aborigines (Australian) The people who lived in Australia before the Europeans. Aborigines now share Australia with people from other countries.

Alloy A mixture of two or more metals.

Archaeologists People who study objects and remains from ancient times before people began to record history.

Artifacts Objects made by humans such as tools or works of art, especially objects of archaeological interest.

Bridle Leather device which fits on a horse's head and is used to control its movements.

Bushmen A race of humans living a hunter-gatherer way of life in parts of southern Africa.

Ceramic Made of clay.

Climate The usual, or prevailing, weather conditions of a particular region.

Concentric Having the same center.

Crop The produce of plants sown by humans for food. Wheat, carrots and potatoes are all crops.

Domestic animals An animal is said to be domestic if it lives together with humans — the opposite of a wild animal. Cows, pigs and dogs are all domestic.

Domestication The act of turning a wild species of animal into a domestic species.

Evolution The continuous change and development of plant or animal species as they adapt to their environment over a long period of time.

Excavate To dig up.

Fertile Land is said to be fertile if it produces large crops each year.

Fortifications Walls and trenches built to strengthen a position.

Fossil The remains or impressions of early life forms preserved in the layers of the earth.

Germinate To begin to grow or develop. To sprout; put forth shoots.

Glacier A large mass of ice which starts from a build-up of snow in a high valley and slowly moves down a mountain.

Ice Age A period of time when a large part of the earth's surface was covered with ice.

Irrigation The watering of land by means of canals or water pipes.

Maoris A Polynesian people; original inhabitants of New Zealand.

Memorial Something intended to remind people of a person or an event.

Navigators People who steer or direct the course of a ship or a plane.

Paleolithic Of the "Old Stone Age" — characterized by the use of stone tools.

Prehistoric Belonging to the time before history was written or records were kept.

Prey Animals that are hunted and killed for food.

Sickle Curved tool used to cut grain crops by hand.

Temples Buildings where people gather to worship a god or gods.

Threshing The act of separating grain from stalks by hitting or tossing the stalks.

Urban Having to do with a city or town.

Books to Read

Benton, Michael **The Story of Life on Earth** (Franklin Watts, 1986).

Cooke, Jean **Archaeology,** *Updated Edition* (Warwick, 1982).

Jaspersohn, William **How People First Lived** (Franklin Watts, 1985).

Lampton, Christopher **New Theories on the Origins of the Human Race** (Franklin Watts, 1989)

Sauvain, Philip **How History Began** (Warwick, 1985).

Index

Picture Acknowledgments

The pictures in this book were supplied by: Brian and Cherry Alexander 8;
Chapel Studios 17; Bruce Coleman: John Fennell 5, Jennifer Fry 16 (top),
Peter Ward 16 (bottom), Gerald Cubitt 17 (bottom right), Hans Reinhard 17
(top left), M.P.L. Fogden 17 (top right), Giorgio Gualco 17 (bottom);
Topham 4, 7, 20 (both); ZEFA 6, 14.